IN AND AROUND
BATH

Built around Britain's only natural hot mineral springs, Bath has been a spa town for 2,000 years. The gushing thermal waters, thought to have great healing powers, are said to have originated as rainwater which fell on the Mendip Hills. The water rises from a depth of 3,000 metres (10,000ft) at over one million litres (220,000 gallons) a day and remains at a constant temperature of 46°C, reaching the surface in three places in the city centre. Designated a World Heritage Site, Bath, steeped in Roman and Georgian history, is a favoured destination for visitors worldwide.

ROMAN BATHS

Legend says that the Celtic Prince Bladud, father of King Lear, founded Bath in 863BC after being banished from court and disowned by his father for contracting leprosy. Seeking a living as a swineherd, he fled to the hot marshy springs in Swainswick, where Bath now stands. His pigs so enjoyed wallowing in the warm mud that they had to be enticed out with acorns and Bladud noticed that their warts and lesions had disappeared. He, too, covered himself in mud and, where it touched his bare skin, he also was cured. Bladud's small statue can be seen in the Roman baths and acorns can now be spotted on stonework in tribute to the ancient king.

Water Source

A large flat slab of stone, known today as the diving stone, lies where hot water flows into the Great Bath.

Great Bath

The centrepiece of the Roman bathing establishment was the Great Bath, fed with hot water directly from the sacred spring.

The conquering Romans were the first to use the hot waters for their own purposes. In around AD65, using engineering techniques ahead of their time, they built a temple and baths around the sacred spring that remains at the very heart of the ancient monument. On the north side there was a fountain fed by a lead pipe from the sacred spring, later replaced with a small monument with a hole to allow a pipe through.

Measurements

Lined with 45 sheets of thick lead and 1.6 metres (5ft) deep, the Great Bath is accessed by four steep steps surrounding it.

ROMAN BATHS

Circular Bath

Unearthed in 1880, the Circular Bath's cold water would close the pores of bathers and was known as the frigidarium.

The city became a religious shrine and bathing spa where bathers, many of whom would travel miles to experience the waters, rubbed oil into their skin and then acclimatized to the heat by moving from a tepid steam room into a hot room. This specially heated room was known as a *laconicum* and could be turned into a steam room by splashing water around. Bathers would quickly break out in a profuse sweat after just a few minutes. Afterwards they would plunge into the invigorating cold circular bath, a feature of many Roman bathhouses, but hardly ever seen on this grand scale. The bath is 1.6 metres (5ft) deep and on one side has an underwater plinth where once a fountain would have been. Warm water was always difficult and expensive to produce, but at Bath the Romans had discovered a surfeit and used it to luxuriate and even swim in the large bathing area at their leisure.

Coins

Almost 20,000 coins and several gold and silver artefacts from the Roman era have been recovered .

The water became renowned for its healing powers and pilgrims believed throwing coins and personal belongings into the spring meant they could communicate directly with the underworld. There are inscribed dedications, vows and curses, many written on thin rolled-up pewter sheets. One says, 'Let him buy it back with his life or his own blood.' Others appealed to a lost love or asked for a culprit to meet an unpleasant end.

The springs were dedicated to the goddess Minerva, originally the Celtic goddess Sulis, whose gilded bronze face once glared down from her statue inside the classical temple and after whom the city, Aqua Sulis, was named. She was later dismembered, probably by Christians suspicious of her pagan power. Any water not required for bathing went via the spring overflow towards the great Roman drain. It was wood-lined, large enough to stand in, and still works perfectly well today, directing the water into the nearby River Avon.

Gorgon's Head

The Gorgon, a mythical creature killed by the Greek hero Perseus, had snakes entwined within its beard and wings and above its ears. Its sun-like appearance may refer to the heat of the sacred spring.

5

Once the Romans left, the baths fell into disrepair until the 11th century when Bishop John de Villula built the King's Bath for the sick, over the top of the original spring. It provided places for bathers to sit, immersed up to their necks in water. On the south side is a seat beneath the waterline, known as the Master of the Baths' chair. The West Baths contain an exceptionally well-preserved set of *pilae*, piles of tiles which allow hot air to circulate to heat the room above. The Victorians rediscovered the baths during the 1860s and excavated the site, now 6 metres (18ft) lower than the rest of the city. In 1894 they added their own statues of Roman governors of Britain and military leaders around the terrace that overlooks the Great Bath. The below-ground Roman Baths museum houses amazing archaeological and historical collections including finds from the Roman Temple such as the Roman 'sea beasts' mosaic, illustrating mythical sea creatures, the front part horse, the rear fish. Blue, red and brown coloured pieces of stone and tiles known as tesserae make up the creatures.

King's Bath

The King's Bath was constructed using the lower walls of the Roman spring building as foundations.

Mosaic

The 'sea beasts' mosaic was discovered in 1859 on the site of the Bluecoat School in Sawclose, central Bath.

Sacred Spring

Roman engineers built the lead-lined sacred spring to supply water to the baths.

Rings

*Signet rings from
2,000 years ago,
made from gem-
stones with portraits
of animals, birds
and gods, were often
used as seals.*

Head of Minerva

*The precious
historical relic,
Minerva's Head,
lay undiscovered
for over 1,000
years before being
uncovered by
workmen in 1727
when digging a
sewage trench.*

BATHS

THERMAE BATH SPA

Roof-top pool

There are bubbling airbeds within the pool, while beyond are breathtaking views over Bath.

F ive historic buildings, including the 18th-century listed buildings Hot Bath and Cross Bath, were restored to create the Thermae Bath Spa which opened to the public in 2006. The project saw the building of the stunning glass and stone New Royal Bath, built on the site of the 1920s Beau Street swimming baths. The main entrance is in Bath Street and the designers complemented the city's Georgian architecture by making good use of circular and curved shapes, and cladding the cube-shaped building in natural Bath stone ties it in with the surroundings. The spa draws water from the King's Spring, the Cross Bath and the Hetling Spring, a bore hole sunk in 1998. A computerized monitoring system ensures that flow of water and temperature information is available at all times. The site has natural thermal baths at Cross Bath and in the New Royal Bath, including a very popular all-year-round open-air rooftop pool with skyline views across Bath, spectacular during the day and magical at twilight. Amongst other facilities there are aroma steam rooms with a central waterfall shower, the grand Minerva Bath, plus all types of treatments including various hot stone massages and luxury thermae facials, and a host of special spa packages. Refreshments are available, daytime and evening, in the Springs Café Restaurant. The free Spa Visitor Centre, a few steps away from Thermae Bath Spa, has interactive displays and exhibits portraying the role the spa waters have played in the history of the city.

Thermae Bath Spa

The spa building which houses the main complex is surrounded by a translucent glass-fronted exterior.

Cross Bath

The natural spring waters rise and fall freely from the poolside fountain, specially designed by renowned water sculpturist William Pye.

BATH ABBEY

Standing at the very heart of the city of Bath for over 12 centuries, Bath's impressive Abbey is now the third church to occupy this site. An Anglo-Saxon abbey church dating from 757, the first to be built, was pulled down by the Norman conquerors of England soon after 1066. A huge Norman cathedral, begun about 1090, proved to be too expensive for the monastery to maintain and by the end of the 15th century it lay in ruins. In 1499 the Bishop of Bath and Wells, Oliver King, was said to have seen, in a dream, angels going up and down a ladder near the foot of an olive tree. He heard a voice say, 'Let an Olive establish the Crown and let the King restore the church.' He had previously been imprisoned by King Richard III, but was now in a position of some power and set about raising the necessary finances to pull down the old and ruined Norman church and build a replacement. Oliver King's signature can be seen on the front of the Abbey while an olive tree, surrounded by the king's crown, has been carved onto the two outer buttresses. A cleaning and conservation programme, undertaken in 2000, revealed the contours and the true colour of the Bath stone from which the Abbey is constructed.

Abbey Courtyard

With views of the west front, the Abbey Courtyard is popular with visitors.

The Abbey

Bath Abbey, built
in restrained
Perpendicular style,
has a tower that
rises to 49 metres
(161ft).

Stained Glass

The Abbey's 52
windows are filled
with exquisite
stained glass,
mostly from the
Victorian era.

ABBEY

BATH
ABBEY

Entertainers

*The Abbey
Courtyard has long
been associated with
street entertainers.*

West Front

The imposing west front; a statue of Henry VII, the first Tudor king, can be seen above the solid oak doors.

The Abbey's stained-glass windows take up almost 80 per cent of the building's wall space. Beneath the west window are scenes from the Old Testament, while at the opposite end of the long nave is the great east window, containing 76 square metres (91sq ft) of glass, depicting Jesus's life from the New Testament. So much light shone out from the church in the days before street lighting, it lit the surrounding area and was affectionately called 'The Lantern of the West'. The magnificent 24-metre (79-ft) high fan-vaulted ceiling above the nave contains armorial carving between the fans. Around 100 heraldic shields decorate the ceiling vaults, including the Abbey's own coat of arms. Other examples of fine carving can be found in the Abbey's chantry, built by William Birde, Prior of Bath from 1499 to 1525. The wall of the north aisle is crammed with many of the Abbey's 640 memorial wall tablets commemorating worshippers at Bath, such as clergyman Thomas Malthus (1766–1834) and Thomas Pownall (1722–1805), the Governor of Massachusetts in America.

Angels

As seen in a vision by Bishop King, angels climb up and tumble headfirst down the ladder between earth and heaven.

On Whit Sunday 973, Edgar, Prince of the royal house of Wessex and King of Mercia, was crowned ruler of all England in the Anglo-Saxon Abbey Church. The order of service devised for Edgar's crowning has been the basis of coronations for monarchs of England ever since. The Edgar Window at the east end of the Abbey depicts the ceremony, conducted by St Dunstan and St Oswald. A stone in the floor in the chancel marks the visit in 1973 of Queen Elizabeth II and Prince Philip, to commemorate the 1,000th anniversary of Edgar's crowning.

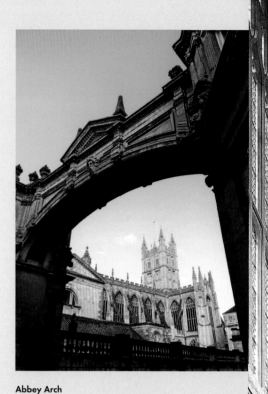

Altar Frontal

The Gethsemane frontal commemorates those who died when the city was bombed during the Second World War and the present-day support for Amnesty International.

Abbey Arch

Heads of sheep and goats decorate York Street Arch and disguise pipework encased within the stone.

Bath Abbey offers Tower Tours, when visitors can see the building from a totally different perspective by seeing the ringing chamber and bell chamber, standing on top of the vaulted ceiling and going behind the clock face. The tour involves ascending 212 steps to the top of the tower, via two spiral staircases – but there is an opportunity to rest during the journey. The ascent is well worthwhile for, on reaching the roof, those who climbed this high get the most magnificent view across the city and into the countryside beyond.

Nave

The nave was restored in the 1860s, with a striking vaulted ceiling made from local stone and modelled on the original Tudor designs by King Henry VII's master masons, William and Robert Vertue.

PUMP ROOM

Drawing Water

Many people still come to drink the water at Bath, in the hope it will cure common ailments.

The first Pump Room was built in the style of an orangery and begun in 1704, taking two years to build before being extended in 1751. It was taken down and rebuilt in its entirety in 1796 to accommodate the increasing number of visitors flocking to Bath. Long regarded as the social heart of Bath with its double-storey windows, high ceilings and crystal chandeliers, it provides a light and sophisticated, yet restful, place to lunch and drink natural spring water from the hot spa, which is often served by a pumper in costume reminiscent of 1795.

King's Spring

After the installation of the King's Spring in 1661, it became fashionable to drink water for its redeeming properties.

THE KING'S SPRING

16

Pump Room

Enjoy a light lunch or high tea in the elegant, spacious and relaxing surroundings of the Pump Room.

The present Pump Room was designed by Thomas Baldwin in 1789. Here, in the early 18th century, Georgian aristocracy would meet for lunch and drink the recommended three glasses of water a day as a health cure, although on doctor's orders some imbibed as much as a gallon. Today many hundreds of people still come to sample the refreshments, although the warm spa waters have a high calcium and sulphate content and an unusual taste, which is not to everyone's palate. It contains 43 minerals, and is still believed by some to have curative properties. The Pump Room contains a number of curiosities, including a selection of sedan chairs and the Tompion clock, given to the city in 1709 by Thomas Tompion, England's best-known clockmaker. Musical accompaniment is provided by either a pianist or the Pump Room Trio, the oldest resident ensemble in Europe, who play every day throughout the year. Music from the cello, piano and violin creates a wonderful atmosphere in which to relax.

Pump Room

Look out for the Greek inscription above the entrance that translates as 'Water is best'.

Queen Square, begun in 1729, is named after Queen Caroline, wife of King George II. In 1702, 27 years earlier, Queen Anne, suffering from dropsy, visited Bath to take the waters in an attempt to find a cure. This started a trend, aided by the flamboyant Welshman Richard 'Beau' Nash, who was appointed Master of Ceremonies in 1706. As well as having a liking for an extravagant dress style and eight mistresses, he established Bath as one of the most fashionable places to be seen.

The obelisk in the square celebrates the 1738 visit of Frederick, Prince of Wales. It was designed by architect John Wood, and financed by Beau Nash, with the stone donated from the quarry belonging to Ralph Allen. During the 18th century, the three men provided the style, social tone and stone for the city, giving Bath its unique reputation. Beau Nash imposed law and order on the city, even laying down strict rules on the sedan chair owners, which became the foundations for governing today's taxis. In Queen's Parade Place there are two small gatehouses marking the spot where gentry would find a sedan chair, to save their weary legs from walking the city's hills.

The Herschel Museum of Astronomy in New King Street is on the site where

Queen Square

Completed in 1736, Queen Square is designed to look like an enormous grand house rather than the seven separate town houses it actually is.

Telescope

A replica of William Herschel's 'seven-foot Newtonian reflecting telescope', with side eyepiece, the original of which he used to discover the planet Uranus in 1781.

William Herschel discovered the planet Uranus in March 1781. Not only did William and his sister Caroline make important discoveries about the solar system, but both were gifted musicians as well. The Grade II listed building, set over five floors, has been restored in the authentic style of the period, with details of wallpaper coming from fragments discovered in Bath houses and the carpets being to an original 18th-century design.

Bath has been home to several theatres since the first small and cramped theatre was built in 1705 by George Trim. Stonemasons' carvings are still in evidence today, as seen in Trim Street, dating back to this very period. The Theatre Royal in Sawclose has been on its present site since 1805 and undergone several renovations over the years, most recently of the main theatre in 2010. It reopened with a production of *The Rivals*, directed by Peter Hall and starring Penelope Keith and Peter Bowles.

Nearby, the Jane Austen Centre tells the story of the writer, who lived in Bath from 1801 to 1806 and used her knowledge of the city to write two of her novels, *Northanger Abbey* and *Persuasion*. The city is still much as Jane Austen knew it. Her father's grave is in St Swithin's churchyard and her aunt lived in a house on the Paragon. In Merchant's House, at the corner of Gay Street and Old King Street, is a powder room where the aristocracy would pause to powder their wigs.

Theatre Royal

In 1768 a royal patent was given to Bath granting a Theatre Royal, the first bestowed outside London.

ROYAL CRESCENT

Bath has eight crescents but Royal Crescent is the most spectacular. The legacy of John Wood the Younger, it was built between 1767 and 1774 and is one of the finest examples of Palladian architecture in Bath, and indeed the world. The 152-metre (500-ft) semi-elliptical terrace, with over 100 Ionic columns, resembles a seemingly endless grand palace. The John Wood father and son architectural partnership shaped Bath by their design and enthusiasm for the city. Passionate about returning Bath to its Roman roots, Wood the Elder planned a forum, circus and gymnasium. His plans were changed but his vision remains in his designs for The Circus and the Assembly Rooms. The Wood's family trademark remains to this day that of imposing terraces of grand townhouses looking like impressive country homes, surrounded by beautifully landscaped settings. Typically, a Bath house has a Welsh slate roof, stone façade, elegant sash windows and a large wooden front door.

Royal Crescent

The sweeping majesty of Royal Crescent was the first of its kind in the world and has been copied many times since. The open space surrounding it gives the illusion of a fine palace set in vast grounds.

Royal Victoria Park

Royal Crescent can be glimpsed through the colourful flower displays in Royal Victoria Park.

Gravel Walk

Just like Anne and Captain Wentworth in Jane Austen's Persuasion, *visitors to Bath can enjoy the chance of a good conversation while strolling along Gravel Walk.*

Inspiration

The composer Haydn thought Royal Crescent 'magnificent'. It is said to have been inspired by the colonnade surrounding Rome's Piazza S. Pietro.

Ralph Allen was a self-made man known as the 'Man of Bath', who became the city's mayor in 1742. After arriving penniless from Cornwall and sheltering as a homeless young boy, he was spotted by a local postmaster who offered him a job. Allen went on to reorganize the postal service in Bath, and used the money to buy the quarries at Combe Down where limestone was mined. Much of the stone used in buildings around the city comes from Allen's quarries, despite it being earlier rejected for building Greenwich Hospital in London because it was considered too soft. Allen used it to build his country home, Prior Park, and died a much-respected wealthy man.

Dining Room

The furniture and decor of No.1 Royal Crescent reflect the period and grandeur of the house which remains one of the finest examples of Palladian architecture in the city.

The foundation stone for No.1 Royal Crescent (now a World Heritage Building) was laid in 1767 and its first resident, Thomas Brock, moved in two years later. The Duke of York, second son of George III, soon followed and 'engaged the first house in the Royal Crescent' in 1776. By 1968, 'Number 1' was a boarding house and in need of much work. Major Bernard Cayzer, a member of the famous shipping family, acquired the house and donated it to the Bath Preservation Trust. Using materials appropriate to the 18th century, they returned the rooms to their former grandeur, featuring authentic fittings, furniture, paintings and carpets. Another major redevelopment project was completed in 2013, reconnecting the main house to its original service wing at No.1a. The extended museum now includes a Georgian Shop on the ground floor, inspired by 18th-century designs of shops in Bath.

The Georgian Garden off Gravel Walk is the country's first 18th-century town garden ever recreated. Situated behind a house in The Circus, it follows an original formal layout, with three flower beds on a central axis, surrounded by gravel and a long bed at the end.

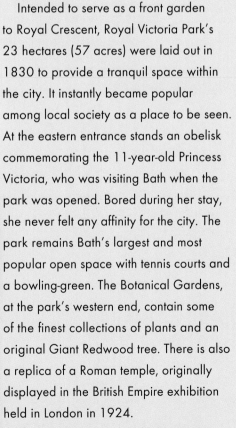

Lady's Bedroom

A door to the service staircase from the lady's bedroom allowed maids to bring water, coal and other necessities when required.

Botanical Gardens

The replica Roman temple in the Botanical Gardens beyond which, in the western corner, lies an aviary.

Intended to serve as a front garden to Royal Crescent, Royal Victoria Park's 23 hectares (57 acres) were laid out in 1830 to provide a tranquil space within the city. It instantly became popular among local society as a place to be seen. At the eastern entrance stands an obelisk commemorating the 11-year-old Princess Victoria, who was visiting Bath when the park was opened. Bored during her stay, she never felt any affinity for the city. The park remains Bath's largest and most popular open space with tennis courts and a bowling-green. The Botanical Gardens, at the park's western end, contain some of the finest collections of plants and an original Giant Redwood tree. There is also a replica of a Roman temple, originally displayed in the British Empire exhibition held in London in 1924.

The gardens also include the Great Dell, a disused quarry developed into a woodland garden which contains an excellent collection of conifers and an abundance of beautiful plants.

23

THE CIRCUS

The Circus

The magnificent mathematical symmetry of The Circus. The columns on the façade show the three styles of classical architecture: Doric, Ionic and Corinthian.

Startlingly symmetrical, The Circus is a perfect circle of 33 houses in three blocks entered by three separate streets. Designed in 1754 as an inverted replica of the Roman Colosseum, it was unique in town planning and completed in 1767 by John Wood the Younger after the death of his father. It originally included a large paved centre as a huge open space, but this has now been softened by lawn and a collection of plane trees with branches kept low to enable the complete circle to be viewed from any point. The houses are designed with great attention to detail, including elegant iron railings, twin columns on each storey, and a decorative frieze, all crowned with delicately carved stone acorns on the parapet. Famous residents have included Thomas Gainsborough who rented No.17 while painting *Blue Boy*, and William Pitt the Elder, MP and Prime Minister, who bought No.7.

Georgian Garden

Situated behind The Circus, the Georgian Garden was discovered by Bath Archaeological Trust in the 1980s almost intact and has been planted with species fitting to the 1760s.

Carving Detail

Running along the top of the Doric columns is a decorated stone frieze featuring the arts, sciences and professions, while friezes on the other levels have been left plain.

GEORGIAN CRESCENTS

Lansdown Crescent

This Crescent is famous for its railings forged into an arch with a lamp to light the way. They must now all be painted black but would originally have been a mix of blue, grey and stone.

The dramatic sight of Cavendish Crescent, with Lansdown Crescent nestling behind it on the Lansdown Slopes, is one of the best views in the city. Poet John Betjeman loved Lansdown Crescent and its adjoining Somerset Place, admiring it as 'without equal as a spectacular townscape'.

Cavendish Crescent's simple symmetry comes from architect John Pinch's design. Somerset Place took 30 years to complete and has the only split pediment in the city at the top of the building. Damaged at the west end during the war, it has now been rebuilt.

Cavendish Crescent

The four-storey Cavendish Crescent is plainer in style than the other crescents in Bath.

Camden Crescent sits high above the eastern side of the city and is the first view of Bath when arriving by train from London. Built during the 1790s, there were many landslides on the site leading to the demolition of the north-eastern end. This accounts for the off-centre appearance of the crescent. John Wood had great plans for North and South Parade, a very tricky site on Abbey Orchard. He wanted to build a 'Royal Forum' that would rival Queen Square, but sadly only a small section was ever completed. Problems with builders and drainage meant his dream was never realized.

Margaret's Buildings

A shoppers' paradise, Margaret's Buildings features leading names in fashion, design and jewellery.

Margaret Garrard, the wife of Sir Benet Garrard who owned the land on which Royal Crescent and Brock Street were built, gave her name to the street called Margaret's Buildings. Shops such as milliners and booksellers sprang up through trade from the passing gentry, with rooms above often let to visitors. Today, there are galleries and eateries here, as well as shops.

CRESCENTS

FESTIVALS AND SHOWS

Bath's festivals make the city buzz with excitement all year round. In early spring, the renowned Literature Festival entertains readers and writers in various venues around the city. In March, thousands of runners take to the streets for the Half Marathon Race. In late spring/early summer, the whole city hosts the International Music Festival, with an eclectic mix of jazz, classical, folk and contemporary sounds. May also sees the popular Bathfest, held at Bath race course – every year offers something new. Around the end of May the Royal Bath and West Show takes place at nearby Shepton Mallet, with livestock, competitions, displays, food and drink, trade stands and activities for children. At the Fringe Festival during late spring/early summer, all art forms come together to perform. With the height of summer comes the International Guitar Festival and the Love Bath City Festival.

Literature Festival

Mr Tickle visits the Children's Literature Festival.

Music Festival

A stunning firework display lights up Royal Victoria Park during the International Music Festival.

Jane Austen Festival

Jane Austen characters come to life on the streets of Bath, and visitors can follow in the author's footsteps.

As summer turns to autumn, there is the Jane Austen Festival. Such is the interest in the writer that there is a week of book readings, concerts, tours, talks and workshops in the city. At October's Great Bath Feast, chefs work with suppliers to create seasonal, locally sourced menus, and you can walk the Bath Taste Trail sampling flavours at different locations. Another autumn favourite is the Children's Literature Festival, when young book fans can meet favourite authors and literary characters.

Music Festival

A baroque procession in the heart of the city at Bath's International Music Festival.

In the latter part of the year, Bath again bursts into activity with its Film Festival, featuring screenings and workshops at several different locations. During November, the classical music extravaganza 'Mozartfest' has performances at such locations as the Assembly Rooms, Guildhall, Bath Abbey and the Forum. At the Christmas Market, the city streets see 150 traditional wooden chalets offering unique, handmade and unusual gifts, decorations and food items in a winter wonderland.

The Ballroom

Built at a cost of £14,000, the Assembly Rooms were opened with a 'Grand Ridotto' whereby a one-guinea ticket would provide entrance for one gentleman and two ladies!

Completed in 1771 by John Wood the Younger, the Assembly Rooms were the centre of Georgian elite society where they could go to dance, gamble or exchange gossip. The Octagon, used for card playing, has four fireplaces for extra warmth. On Sundays, when cards were forbidden, people would sit and listen to the organ in the musicians' gallery. During balls held at the Assembly Rooms, ladies would cool off and gossip about dancing partners in so-called 'corridors of scandal'.

Dances

Assembly Rooms balls were colourful affairs, full of intrigue and gossip, and the chance to see and be seen.

Fashion Museum

Exhibits in the museum are regularly changed so there is always something new to see, such as this elegant 1950s ballgown.

By the 1850s the social scene had gone into decline and the Assembly Rooms fell into disuse. They were converted into a cinema in the 1920s, before becoming the property of The National Trust. Extensive work after the Second World War restored the building to its former glory. In the Assembly Rooms is the Fashion Museum, the creation of Doris Langley Moore, a designer and historian who donated her private collection to the city. Exhibits include fashions from Georgian and Victorian times right through to the most recent 'dress of the year'.

UPPER TOWN

Upper Town has a wealth of museums. The Museum of Bath at Work uses artefacts as diverse as steam engines, corsets and Second World War gas masks, to tell the story of Bath's commercial and industrial heritage, cleverly integrated into how the city evolved socially. By reconstructing Jonathan Bowler's Victorian family-run business, it gives a unique insight into the workings of a company that used the owner's many talents to do everything, from making locks and hanging bells to repairing soda-water machinery.

The Building of Bath Collection was opened in 1992 by the Bath Preservation Trust and is housed in the Countess of Huntingdon's Chapel in The Paragon. This unique collection celebrates the colourful architectural history of the city, and the craftsmen who turned it into the capital of Georgian society. Opened in 2014, the Countess's Room is dedicated to the history of the building and to Selina Hastings, the devout Countess who in 1765 had the chapel built in protest against the decadence of Georgian Bath. Also within this Grade II listed building, the only complete 18th-century Gothic Revival building in Bath, is the Bath City Model, a detailed 1:500 scale architectural model of the layout of the Georgian city centre. Here, too, is the Bath Buildings Record, viewable by appointment. This project records details and images of the buildings destined for demolition during modernisation of the city in the 1960s and 1970s.

Museum of Bath at Work

A faithful reconstruction of the shop and offices of Jonathan B. Bowler, using materials removed from the original 1872 premises in Corn Street, can be investigated here.

Museum of East Asian Art

A 17th-century (Qing dynasty) Chinese wucai (five-coloured) jar decorated with a banquet scene.

Chair Legs

These delicate Georgian chair legs, from the Building of Bath Collection, were made from cheaper native woods and painted to imitate more desirable materials such as bamboo.

Based in a restored Georgian building, the Museum of East Asian Art houses a fine and colourful collection of Chinese, Japanese, Korean and South-East Asian treasures. The objects date from around 5000BC to the present day and reveal the finest achievements in East Asian craftsmanship. With its emphasis on promoting a deeper understanding of East Asian cultures through education, the museum has a lifelong commitment to learning, with an award-winning educational programme for children, plus a programme of events for adults.

TOWN CENTRE

Milsom Street is one of Bath's most famous, elegant and fashionable shopping streets and is home to one of the country's oldest and most prestigious department stores, Jolly's, now owned by the House of Fraser. Opened in 1831 by Mr James Jolly as the Bath Emporium, a carved stone, granite and mahogany shop front was added in 1879. A copy of the Magna Carta is reproduced on a long wall behind the store.

Together with New Bond Street, Milsom Street comprises a lovely fashion quarter in Bath. About halfway up Milsom Street is the entrance to Shire's Yard, which is full of delightful shops to explore.

The names of Quiet, John and Wood Streets refer to a council meeting where John Wood the Elder became passionate about the naming of a set of streets and demanded to be given an answer. In no uncertain terms the chairman snapped back, 'Quiet, John Wood!' Taking him at his word, the three streets were named accordingly. On John Street are Paxton and Whitfield, renowned for specialist cheeses.

One of the more famous guests at 'The Saracen's Head' in Broad Street was author Charles Dickens, who stayed there in 1835 during his time as a political reporter in the city when he was covering a speech by Lord Russell.

Shire's Yard

The buildings in Shire's Yard are almost unchanged since Walter Wiltshire built the stables in the 1740s to house his 'flying wagons', which took almost three days to reach London.

New Bond Street Place

This small alleyway of shops offers a welcome contrast to high-street stores.

Victoria Art Gallery

John Nash's c.1927 oil painting shows Canal Bridge in Sydney Gardens. It forms part of the Victoria Art Gallery's wonderful collection of art.

In Northgate Street is the Bath Postal Museum, which explores 4,000 years of communication. The museum celebrates the fact that the city played a vital role in the development of communications, and improving the British postal service. Here you can learn about the men who were key players in setting up the Post Office, and the history of the traditional post box.

Bath Postal Museum

The first stamp in the world, the Penny Black, was posted from Bath on 2 May 1840.

Playwright Richard Sheridan's comedies, *The Rivals* and *School for Scandal* are set in Bath where he lived. He eloped with the 17-year-old singer Elizabeth Linley, and they fled from her home in Royal Crescent to France. Sheridan then was forced to duel with another of his wife's admirers, as their marriage remained a secret from her father.

Architectural Detail

The Guildhall was built in 1777 to much acclaim and is a masterpiece of neo-classical decoration.

Sally Lunn, a young French refugee, came to England over 300 years ago and started to bake a large, round, satisfying bread, which became known as the Sally Lunn Bun. It was renowned for its compatibility with either sweet or savoury food. She carried them round the streets offering them to hungry customers. Today her shop, situated in North Passage Parade and the oldest property in Bath, still bakes the buns following the same secret recipe Sally used all those years ago. The cellars house a small museum as well as showing the Roman and medieval foundations to the house. The original kitchen has a Georgian range and baking equipment. Round the corner, on the south side of York Street, an iron gateway can be seen leading down some steps to the distinctive Palladian-style home of Ralph Allen.

Guildhall

Designed by city architect Thomas Baldwin in the 1770s, the Guildhall has spectacular chandeliers, a musicians' gallery and features portraits of many of Bath's famous citizens.

Nelson and his mistress Lady Hamilton (who as a girl served at the home of composer Thomas Linley) stayed in Bath on many occasions, and lived at 88 Pierrepont. His first visit was in 1781 after an overseas tour left him weak and unwell and he felt the need to take the healing waters. The Crystal Palace pub, behind the Abbey in Abbey Green, dates back to 1654 and is well known for its spectacular floral displays.

Opened in 2009, Bath's newest shopping centre, SouthGate, was built on the site of the old bus station, which is now situated west of Bath Spa railway station. SouthGate was designed to fit in with the Georgian architecture characteristic of the city, with a façade of Bath stone. As well as a great selection of shops, part of the complex is Brunel Square, set amidst Brunel's railway arches and overlooking an open piazza surrounded by eateries.

DOWN BY THE RIVER

Pulteney Bridge

*The three-arched
Pulteney Bridge was
designed by architect
Robert Adam and
is one of only four
bridges in the world
lined with shops.*

Wealthy landowner and Member of Parliament William Pulteney hoped to develop his 243 hectares (600 acres) of potentially prime real estate across the River Avon in Bathwick, with help from Robert Adam. He commissioned a bridge, which Adam proposed should have 11 small shops on each side, with staircases to attics above. The prospect of the bridge paying for itself through shop rents immediately appealed to Pulteney's love of economy. However, despite the bridge's completion in 1774, tenants were slow to come forward and plans for Bathwick were shelved, apart from a small section which included Great Pulteney Street with Sydney Gardens, a place often visited by Jane Austen from her home at 4 Sydney Place. In January 1936, Pulteney Bridge was designated a national monument. Then, in 1975, the Georgian Group partially restored the southern street façade to mark European Architectural Heritage Year.

Nearby Parade Gardens, along Grand Parade, overlook the River Avon giving fine views of Pulteney Bridge and the weir. The flowers are among some of the finest in the country and there are plenty of places to sit and enjoy the scenery.

Parade Gardens

During the summer months there are regular concerts held in Bath's pretty Parade Gardens.

Henrietta Park

Close to Pulteney Bridge, the park contains a Sensory Garden.

Holburne Museum

The art collection of Sir William Holburne is displayed in the magnificent rooms of Holburne Museum, a former hotel dating from the 18th century.

The Bandstand

With its wonderful view of the park, the bandstand is a lovely place to spend some time and, in warmer weather, entertainment is provided by musicians.

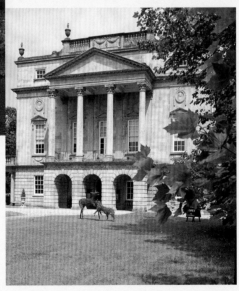

Below Pulteney Bridge and just a few steps away from the horseshoe-shaped weir is the grassed area of Beazer Garden Maze. It has an open-air paved maze leading to a detailed mosaic in the centre and is a popular attraction to young visitors. A few minutes' walk away lies Orange Grove, so called after William of Orange's visit to the city in 1734. The Alkmaar obelisk, named after Bath's twin town in Holland, stands in the circular garden and serves as a reminder of the links between the two countries.

AROUND BATH

The American way of life, from colonial times to the mid-19th-century, is explored at the American Museum in Britain, together with Native American artefacts and galleries devoted to Folk Art. There are 51 hectares (125 acres) of gardens, featuring a replica of George Washington's Mount Vernon garden.

Bath Boating Station is a Victorian boating station on the River Avon with kingfishers, herons, swans and wild geese. Beckford's Tower on Lansdown Hill was built by the eccentric William Beckford, who was determined to leave his mark on Bath. When the tower was about to be completed in 1827, not content with its stature he shouted 'Higher!' and so a lantern was added. He used the building as a retreat and as a home for his precious art collection and rare books. Today, Beckford's Tower and Museum displays prints, pictures, objects and furniture from William's life.

Bath Boating Station

There are traditional wooden skiffs, punts and canoes for hire by the hour or day at Bath Boating Station at Bathwick.

Prior Park

Laid out in the 18th century, Prior Park is set in a sweeping valley with magnificent views of the city.

American Museum

Situated at Claverton, the American Museum in Britain includes the finest collection of American quilts and textiles outside America.

Beckford's Tower

Climbing Beckford's Tower's spiral staircase to the beautifully restored belvedere gives you a chance to admire the panoramic view of the surrounding countryside.

40

Prior Park, now owned by The National Trust, was created by entrepreneur Ralph Allen along with poet Alexander Pope and landscape gardener 'Capability' Brown, and contains a Palladian bridge together with three lakes. A five-minute walk from the garden leads on to the Bath Skyline, an area also owned by The National Trust, comprising woodlands and meadows.

Two miles from the city of Bath, the Kennet and Avon Canal passes through the village of Bathampton, known for its folk-dancing Morris Men, a side founded in 1934, who tour Europe promoting friendship and goodwill. The broad canal opened in 1810 and was built in three sections. Its elegant architecture complements the fertile open plains and rolling downs of the south.

Bathampton

The village lies on the Kennet and Avon Canal, one of the most beautiful waterways in Britain, that snakes across southern England.

Wells

Wells Cathedral is an architectural gem, and has survived through the centuries relatively unscathed.

The stunning cathedral city of Wells lies on the slopes of the Mendip Hills. King Ina of the West Saxons founded the city when he built a church beside the natural water springs. The cathedral, started in 1180, was built to the north of the previous church and is a fine example of early English architecture with its great west front, chapter house and unusual strainer or scissor arches.

The vibrant and exciting city of Bristol lies on the River Avon. The rambling old shipping warehouses at the Watershed have been converted into modern cafés, restaurants and bars. There are several highly popular shopping areas in and around Bristol, including Bristol Shopping Quarter, Park Street and Clifton Village, with outlets to suit all tastes. Thousands of visitors come to stroll across the superbly engineered suspension bridge for views of the gorge and elegant Clifton below.

Bradford-on-Avon's most famous landmark, the bridge, has a room with two cells, iron beds and no windows. It is called a 'blind house' because when inmates awoke in the dark they believed they had lost their sight. Weavers' cottages cling to the side of the Avon valley, looking down across the old mills to the 'Broad Ford' on the river, which gives the town its name.

Bradford-on-Avon

A 12th-century Norman church stands at the heart of Bradford-on-Avon.

Bristol

The Clifton Suspension Bridge, set on the cliffs of the Avon Gorge near Bristol, was designed by the great Victorian engineer Isambard Kingdom Brunel, although he did not live to see it finished.

Tyntesfield

West of Bath, Tyntesfield is a spectacular Victorian Gothic revival house set within lovely grounds, and owned by The National Trust.

Set in more than 364 hectares (900 acres) of parkland landscaped by Capability Brown, with a further 3,238 hectares (8,000 acres) of woodlands, lakes and farmland, Longleat was the first stately home to open its doors to the public and the first place outside Africa to have a safari park, a monkey jungle and sea lions. Sir John Thynne began building the house in 1568 and the flamboyant 7th Marquess of Bath, who passed management of the business to his son in 2010, added a series of murals in the west wing. Longleat also has the world's longest hedge maze with 2.72 kilometres (1.7 miles) of pathways.

The magnificent 18th-century Bowood House has belonged to the Marquess of Landsdowne since 1754, and has been home to the 9th Marquess since 1972. Dr Priestley discovered oxygen in his laboratory here, by observing fish breathing in water. Exhibits include Napoleon's death mask and the glittering Keith jewels. There is a large adventure playground for children, with a life-size pirate ship.

Longleat

Longleat is one of the finest examples of high Elizabethan architecture in Britain. Oranges and lemons are still grown in the Orangery.

Bowood House

The gardens at Bowood House, in Calne, have a cascade, Doric temple, rose gardens and rhododendron walks.

Corsham Court

The original Elizabethan part of Corsham Court was extended by Capability Brown to provide room for its splendid art collection.

Stourhead, near Mere, was one of the first Palladian houses in England and contains furniture by Thomas Chippendale the Younger as well as other works of art. The green-and-white library is one of the best surviving Regency rooms in the country. There are regular guided walks through the outstanding landscaped gardens, which feature a sculptured river god sitting in a lakeside grotto. It is now owned by The National Trust.

Stourhead

A view of the Pantheon, one of a number of classical buildings set around the lake in Stourhead's magnificent grounds which were laid out between 1741 and 1780 by banker Henry Hoare, whose family owned the estate.

Just west of Chippenham lies Corsham Court, a former Saxon royal manor, built in 1582. It is home to the Methuen family and has a renowned collection of 16th- and 17th-century Italian and Flemish Old Master paintings by artists such as Van Dyck, Reynolds and Lippi. The magnificent landscape garden has a rococo-Gothic bath house with a passageway linked to a walled garden. Both house and gardens are regularly used as a film location and appeared in *The Remains of the Day*, which starred Anthony Hopkins and Emma Thompson.

Lacock Abbey

The peace and tranquillity of Lacock Abbey, a former nunnery, is reflected in its architecture. The property is in the care of The National Trust.

Dyrham Park

The 17th-century Bath-stone mansion house of Dyrham Park is full of original furnishings and paintings from Holland, England and America. Dyrham Park is owned by The National Trust.

Lacock Abbey, to the east of Bath, was founded in 1232 and used as an Augustinian nunnery until 1539. The cloisters, chapter house and sacristy were saved when the building was converted into a home in 1550 and later passed to the Talbot family. William Henry Fox Talbot discovered the photographic negative here in 1835 when he took a view of an oriel window in the south gallery. Lacock was the setting for the TV adaptation of Jane Austen's novel *Pride and Prejudice*, as well as the Harry Potter films. Dyrham Park was built between 1691 and 1702 and its ancient deer park, formal gardens and woodlands are used as a concert venue during the summer. Fallow deer roam the beautiful parkland with views across the Bristol Channel to the Welsh mountains.

Westonbirt Arboretum, near Tetbury, started life as an extension of the Holford family estate in 1829. Robert Holford, a wealthy landowner who loved trees and wildlife, began to indulge his passion for botany. Today it has one of the finest tree collections in the world with 18,000 trees from all over the globe, some dating back to 1829, planted in 243 hectares (600 acres) of landscaped countryside. It is managed by the Forestry Commission and has over 29 kilometres (18 miles) of pathways.

Stonehenge is as old as the great temples and pyramids of Egypt. Built in three stages, the first section consisted of a circular ditch and bank, followed by a wooden structure at the centre. The third stage formed the stones seen today. There are two types of stone: the smaller, called Bluestones, hauled from the Preseli mountains in Wales and the larger stones from the Marlborough Downs. In 2013, a brand new visitor centre was opened. Here visitors from all over the world come to enjoy the permanent and temporary exhibitions, the shop and café as part of their visit to see the magnificent stones, which are cared for by English Heritage.

Stonehenge

Stonehenge was built at least 2,000 years ago, perhaps by sun-worshipping pagans.

Westonbirt Arboretum

With 29 kilometres (18 miles) of pathways, this is a beautiful natural habitat for wild flowers, fungi and birds.

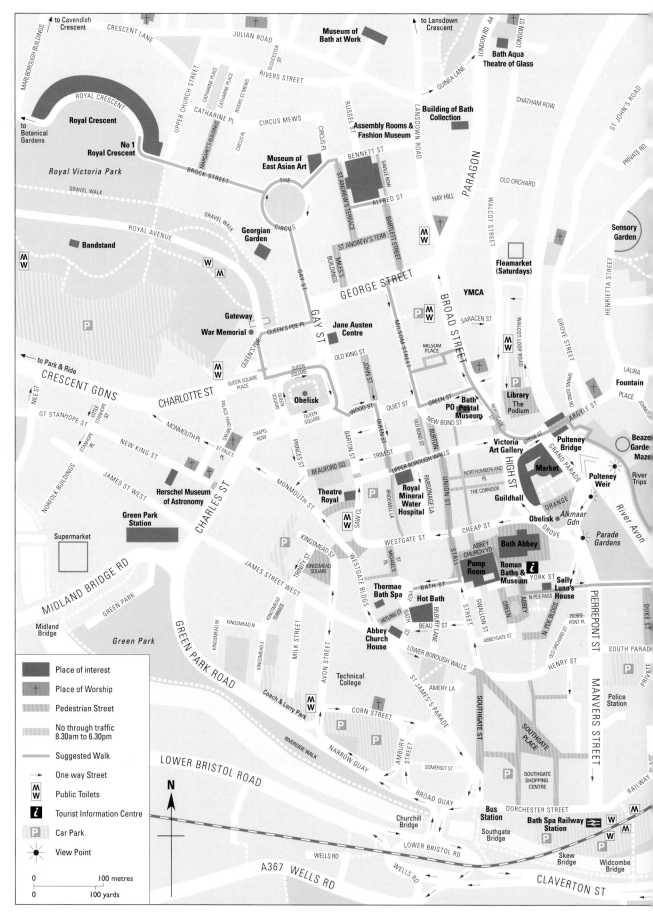

Marlborough Buildings

to Cavendish Crescent

CRESCENT LANE

JULIAN ROAD

Museum of Bath at Work

to Lansdown Crescent

LANSDOWN RD A4

Bath Aqua Theatre of Glass

UPPER CHURCH STREET

CATHARINE PLACE

CATHARINE PL

GLOUCESTER ST

RIVERS STREET

RIVERS ST MEWS

RUSSEL ST

GUINEA LANE

CHATHAM ROW

ST JOHN'S ROAD

ROYAL CRESCENT

Royal Crescent

No 1 Royal Crescent

CIRCUS MEWS

CIRCUS PL

Assembly Rooms & Fashion Museum

LANSDOWN ROAD

Building of Bath Collection

PARAGON

OLD ORCHARD

PRIVATE RD

to Botanical Gardens

BROCK STREET

MARGARET'S BUILDINGS

Museum of East Asian Art

BENNETT ST

ST ANDREW'S TERRACE

SAVILE ROW

ALFRED ST

HAY HILL

WALCOT STREET

Royal Victoria Park

GRAVEL WALK

THE CIRCUS

GAY ST

BARTLETT STREET

Sensory Garden

HENRIETTA STREET

ROYAL AVENUE

GRAVEL WALK

Georgian Garden

ST ANDREW'S TERR

MILES'S BUILDINGS

GEORGE STREET

W M

SARACEN ST

Fleamarket (Saturdays)

YMCA

BROAD STREET

WALCOT LOOP ROAD

GROVE STREET

Bandstand

W M

W

W

Gateway

War Memorial

QUEEN'S PDE PL

Jane Austen Centre

OLD KING ST

MILSOM STREET

MILSOM PLACE

W M

Library

The Podium

SPRING GDNS RD

LAURA PLACE

JOHNSTON

Fountain

P

CRESCENT GDNS

to Park & Ride

NILE ST

W M

CHARLOTTE ST

QUEEN SQUARE PLACE

Queen Square

Obelisk

QUEEN SQUARE

WOOD ST

QUIET ST

JOHN ST

QUEEN ST

GREEN ST

NEW BOND ST

Bath Postal Museum

PO

NORTHGATE

Victoria Art Gallery

BRIDGE ST

GRAND PARADE

Pulteney Bridge

Beazer Garde Maze

River Trips

GT STANHOPE ST

LITTLE STANHOPE ST

STANHOPE PL

PALACE YARD MEWS

ST PAUL'S PL

CHAPEL ROW

PRINCES ST

BEAUFORD SQ

TRIM ST

BARTON ST

OLD BOND ST

BURTON

NORTHUMBERLAND PL

HIGH ST

Market

ARGYLE ST

Pulteney Weir

River Avon

NEW KING ST

MONMOUTH PL

MONMOUTH ST

Herschel Museum of Astronomy

P

Theatre Royal

SAW CL

Royal Mineral Water Hospital

UPPER BOROUGH WALLS

UNION ST

PARSONAGE LA

THE CORRIDOR

Guildhall

Obelisk

Alkmaar Gdn

ORANGE GROVE

Parade Gardens

NORFOLK BUILDINGS

JAMES ST WEST

CHARLES ST

Green Park Station

KINGSMEAD SQUARE

KINGSMEAD ST

BRIDWELL LA

ST MICHAEL'S PL

WESTGATE ST

CHEAP ST

Bath Abbey

ABBEY CHURCH YD

Pump Room

Roman Baths & Museum

STALL ST

GREEN

ABBEY

York St

PIERREPONT ST

DUKE ST

Supermarket

Green Park

MIDLAND BRIDGE RD

JAMES STREET WEST

KINGSMEAD TERRACE

KINGSMEAD N

MILK STREET

TRINITY ST

WESTGATE BLDGS

W M

Thermae Bath Spa

Hot Bath

BATH ST

BEAU ST

BILBURY LANE

SWALLOW ST

Sally Lunn's House

N PDE PASS

PIERREPONT PL

MANVERS STREET

SOUTH PARADE

Midland Bridge

GREEN PARK ROAD

KINGSMEAD W

KINGSMEAD E

Abbey Church House

LOWER BOROUGH WALLS

ABBEYGATE ST

N PDE BLDGS

OLD ORCHARD ST

HENRY ST

Police Station

P

P

PRIVATE

Technical College

AVON STREET

ST JAMES'S PARADE

AMERY LA

SOUTHGATE ST

SOUTHGATE PLACE

SOUTH PARAD

Coach & Lorry Park

W M

CORN STREET

P

NARROW QUAY

AMBURY STREET

SOMERSET ST

SOUTHGATE SHOPPING CENTRE

RIVERSIDE WALK

BROAD QUAY

Bus Station

DORCHESTER STREET

RAILWAY PL

W M

LOWER BRISTOL ROAD

N

Churchill Bridge

Southgate Bridge

Bath Spa Railway Station

W

W

P

A367 WELLS RD

WELLS RD

WELLS RD

LOWER BRISTOL RD

Skew Bridge

Widcombe Bridge

CLAVERTON ST

Legend

	Place of interest
†	Place of Worship
	Pedestrian Street
	No through traffic 8.30am to 6.30pm
	Suggested Walk
→	One way Street
W M	Public Toilets
i	Tourist Information Centre
P	Car Park
●	View Point

0   100 metres
0   100 yards